Tumbling into Light

Tumbling into Light

A Hundred Poems

Richard Bauckham

CANTERBURY
PRESS
Norwich

© Richard Bauckham 2022

First published in 2022 by the Canterbury Press Norwich
Editorial office
3rd Floor, Invicta House
108–114 Golden Lane
London EC1Y OTG, UK
www.canterburypress.co.uk

Canterbury Press is an imprint of Hymns Ancient & Modern Ltd
(a registered charity)

Hymns Ancient & Modern® is a registered trademark of
Hymns Ancient & Modern Ltd
13A Hellesdon Park Road, Norwich,
Norfolk NR6 5DR, UK

A number of these poems have previously appeared in
The Rainbow Poetry News (edited by Hugh Hellicar,
privately published, Shoreham, Sussex).
They are reprinted with permission.

British Library Cataloguing in Publication data

A catalogue record for this book is available
from the British Library

ISBN 978 1 786 22 436 1

Typeset by Regent Typesetting
Printed and bound in Great Britain by
CPI Group (UK) Ltd

Contents

Foreword by Malcolm Guite   xi

The Months

The Colours of January   1
The Colour of February   1
A Moment in March   2
The Colour of April   3
The Colour of May   4
Valerian in June   4
The Colour of July   5
August Light   5
The Colours of September   6
The Colours of October   6
Light in November   7
Trees in December   8

The News from Siberia

The News from Siberia (I)   9
The News from Siberia (II)   10
The News from Siberia (III)   11

Fellow creatures

Twelve Haiku	13
The First Daffodil	15
The Heron	16
The Tree and I	17
Tumbling	18
Angels	19
Trees at Christmas	20
Evening Primrose	20
The Grey Heron	21
Black Holes	21

Poems of the Pandemic

Virus	23
Back to the Future	24
At Christmas in a Pandemic	25
Living with Covid	26

The Church Year

Advent

Haiku for an Advent Calendar	27
Advent	29
Dies Irae	31

Christmas

First Light	32
Song of the Shepherds	33
The Christmas Story	34
The bleary Cows	35
The Adoration	36
Dayspring from on High	36
Approaching Christmas through the Mist	37
Canticles for the Twelve Days of Christmas	38

Epiphany

The Journey of the Magi	39
The Magi tell of their Journey	40
The Star	42
The Magi return to their own Country by another Way	44
The Magi remember	44
'He took the child and his mother by night'	45

Candlemas

Wait and see	46

Ash Wednesday

Ash Wednesday	48

Good Friday

Darkness at Noon	49
Phoenix	50

Easter

Four Women and a Tomb	51
Easter Reverie	52
Early April Flowers	53

Pentecost

A Pentecost Prayer to the Spirit of Life	54

Odes to Francis of Assisi

Il Poverello	55
The Cross at San Damiano	56
A Song for Brother Sun	57
A Song for Sister Moon	58
A Song for Brother Fire	59
A Song for the Most High	60
A Song for Sister Death	61

Tales of the East Neuk

The Isle of May   63
The Blue Stane of Crail   64
The Hermit and the King   65
Saint Fillan   67

Seasons

Five Haiku   69
Premature Spring   70
Spring at last!   70
Dazzled   71
Travelling on   72
Elegy   73

The Sea, the Sea!

Five Haiku   75
The Path to the Sea   76
To Matthew Arnold   77
To Gerard Manley Hopkins   78
The Sounds of Seagulls   79

God

Seven Haiku   81
God!   82
Hide and Seek   83
Reconfiguring   84
At the End of the Day   84

Foreword

by Malcolm Guite

There is deft weaving of interconnected themes in this remarkable debut collection of poetry. A scholar's love and understanding of Scripture is woven together with a poet's love of nature and a feel for what Eliot called 'the present moment of the past'. Figures from the biblical narrative speak to us afresh with contemporary voices, and the voices of the prophets bring ancient insights to the news of the moment.

Though each of these poems can be enjoyed on its own as a distinct and separate lyric, Bauckham has also fashioned them into various sequences which build and develop his major themes.

The first sequence, The Months, revives a tradition that goes back to Spenser's *The Shepherd's Calendar* and has been deftly handled in the twentieth century by John Heath-Stubbs. The key theme here is not just the beauty of nature but the way that beauty, even as it passes, speaks of what is eternal. This is poetry written to 'defy death's brag and lift our eyes / to heed these luscious hints of heaven!'

These lines from 'The Colour of May' also show another aspect of this collection: it is poetry in conversation with both the literary and the biblical traditions. Bauckham's 'darling memories of May' are coloured by Shakespeare's 'darling buds of May', and both poets upbraid death with their glimpse of an 'eternal summer', just as his later poem in that sequence, 'Light in November', makes an airy bridge from nature to liturgy and concludes its own evensong with 'Lighten our darkness, Lord, we pray'.

The next sequence, News from Siberia, introduces another strong theme of this collection: the impact of climate change and the need for a renewed sense of our kinship with and interdependence on all our fellow creatures, a theme to which Bauckham returns and richly develops in his sequences Fellow Creatures and Odes to Francis of Assisi. Though his response to nature is deeply informed by Francis and by poets like Hopkins, to whom he often alludes, his take is not over-romanticized or sentimental. He allows for the utter otherness of nature and also, in a sequence of unsparingly honest poems on the pandemic, he grapples with our dark experiences of the natural world.

Even in the nature poems there are many apt and gentle allusions to the Scriptures, but it is in the central sequence on The Church Year that we find the true meeting of the biblical scholar and the poet. And, as Heaney said of George Mackay Brown, Bauckham 'gives scholarship the kiss of life with a verse'. Again, in this sequence he constantly engages in conversation with the tradition, replying to and reinventing old tropes. So his Advent 'Dies Irae' takes a leaf from the Advent Antiphons and makes a whole new series of cryptic emblems for the coming Christ, not simply the traditional 'Lion of Judah', but also the 'Torch of Liberty', the 'Stone of Destiny', and even the 'Green Man'. Indeed, that verse in his poem renews his ecological theme in an Advent context:

Come soon, Green Man! Re-wild these wastes!
Unfurl your foliage far and wide!

Time and again this sequence refreshes our understanding of Scripture by giving the text a contemporary context. The long wait of Simeon and Anna prompts Bauckham to think of the 'drab waiting-room' of 'failed travellers' in a railway station; the flight into Egypt is placed in the context of 'the trudging millions' of displaced people in our own time.

Bauckham is best known as a distinguished New Testament scholar and theologian, and his scholarly insights discreetly inform and underpin much of this poetry, but he does not turn directly to theology, to speech about God, until the final sequence of this book, and even here he acknowledges the inadequacy of language:

> God is the word that in his absence
> we have borrowed for our own purposes

Perhaps only poetry can face that inadequacy, and by the modest magic of metaphor, do something creative with it. In the poem 'Hide and Seek', Bauckham addresses God and says:

> You are the hidden soul
> of all that matters.
> How could we miss you?

In one sense all the poetry in this collection is attending to that 'hidden soul', helping us, who might have missed it, to catch at least a glimpse.

Malcolm Guite, author of *Sounding the Seasons*

This book is dedicated
to all those who have
liked my poems
and encouraged me
to go on writing them.

THE MONTHS

The Colours of January

Under an ice-blue sky
the frost is a light dusting
that tempers the green of the meadow,
softly blanches the parked punts
and lightens a loaded heart.

The cold feels kindly today,
and a buoyant lightness of being
colours the air with brightness
till the heart floats.

Weightier days will come,
with their important cares,
but today a toddler's fingers tingle,
reaching out, entranced,
to a swan,
snow-white and serene.

The Colour of February

The sky is a ponderous grey
and I recall how, once and for ever,
I trudged bleakly
through sorrow like viscous mud.
It was a landscape leached of colour,
where no one could reach me,
except the one who is always
closer even than damp air or dull pain.

A Moment in March

I pause in this exquisite moment of promise,
as blossoms blushing coyly with just-emerging colour
are waiting to burst their buds,
waiting to enrapture.

It is the moment before Van Gogh,
leaving the dull town and its uncooperative women,
trudges – straw hat and easel strapped to his back
– into his dream of Japan.
Then come delirious days
painting at speed –
his solitary yet soul-sustaining *hanami*.

All that is still to come
as I pause on the cusp
of this pregnant moment.

Before our addiction to instant messaging,
a lover might delay
opening a longed-for letter,
multiplying pleasure
by savouring the anticipation.

Just so, on receipt of this missive from God,
I pause,
content to wait
as I savour his love.

The Colour of April

Walking in paths of peace today,
I wandered through a simmering field
of oil-seed rape, so vast it seemed
to colour all my world and way.

The dandelions at my feet,
cheekily cheerful, led me on.
So doused in yellowness I went
in eager search of my retreat.

There I was ravished by the sight
of cowslips – hundreds, egg-yolk yellow,
massed below the cloudless sky.
Softly they coloured my delight.

I sit here in the still blue air,
while bluebells, cowslips, birdsong meld
into a peace, a healing peace
that with God's creatures I can share.

This peace is not the flabby peace
of ignorance or escape. It is
the strong and sturdy peace God gives
to get us through such times as these.

This churchyard is a sacred space
where death has done its worst and failed.
There is no sadness. Peace, not death,
is the familiar of the place.

So now beside the cowslip host
and names of those I never knew
and some I did, in peace beyond
all understanding I am doused.

The Colour of May

My darling memories of May
are white: the hosts of cow parsley,
the flowing tresses of the queen
of May, the hawthorn, bridal white.
They are the crests of nature's waves.
They brighten every leafy lane
that leads to summer's wedding day.

Such innocence we have betrayed,
trampled and trodden down to build
our roads to nowhere. Spirit of dear life,
sprite of our springtide, Whitsun white,
defy death's brag and lift our eyes
to heed these luscious hints of heaven!
You are the summer that will never fade.

Valerian in June

Deep-pink pagodas of delight –
they greet me every morning like a smile.
On a drab day they sing to me
a morning canticle of heaven's goodwill.
Undesigned they grace my garden
with spontaneous beauty
that is more than beauty,
more the meaning beauty means.

The life they gather into colour
wells up from the generous heart of earth,
and in their blushing blooms
surges to eloquence.

Their gift to me
is simple, pure, intense,
sayable only as blessing.

The Colour of July

We cannot bear the heat of the long day.
We seek out shade – green shade, where green
thoughts grow,
greenness of infinitely various hues,
mottled and musing afternoons away.

Greenness of willow, dock and columbine
soothes our frenetic moods. Stillness pervades.
We drink long draughts of calm to cool our souls.
Silence is human here and song divine.

The strident sunshine, mollified by green,
spatters and spangles, like pure drops of grace,
lighting small candles in our wearied hearts
and scattering sparks of unexpected praise.

August Light

Golden as hope
not disappointed yet
the fields of Fife
gleam in the late sun.
But the poem is elsewhere
where I am not yet.
It is lying there unwritten
in wait for me.
There the tall trees aspire
to hymns of holy light
and the burn burbles
like a child absorbed
in solitary play.

The Colours of September

Autumn winds begin gently
coaxing yellowing leaves
to break free and float,
though many a plump tree still
luxuriates in lively green,
complacent as a cloudless sky,
while, prematurely wizened,
blotched and blighted
leaves of the horse chestnut
drop like slow tears.

The Colours of October

We could say: It's just that trees
are stocking up for winter months.
The colours are mere residue.
They're fooling us if we suppose
that beauty enters into it at all.

Angels know better. In their eyes
the greens of lusty earth transmute
to hues of heaven's aspiring heights,
ardent and luminous with praise,
colours that dance and dazzle in their hearts.

All this ripe glory falls and fades
like tears of angels. To the dust
returns all that is made from dust.
All that we love must fall, and yet
in angels' eyes the glory glows with hope.

Light in November

The cold light clarifies each branch and twig
and falls unsmiling on the frosted grass.
But yellow still and softly bright
the willows bask in the cool light.

Light of the world, you know we cannot bear
unsparing scrutiny of all we are
unless your light is love that drives
each lurking shadow from our lives.

Sometimes your rays elucidate the seer.
Sometimes your kindly light, soft to tired eyes,
heartens the ending of the day.
Lighten our darkness, Lord, we pray.

Trees in December

As the last leaves fall
the trees lay bare a different beauty –
involuted shapes
etched like tattoos
on the pale torso of the sky.

This is their dreamtime.
Lost in reverie,
they sink into themselves
and slow their musings till they reach
their ancient stillness.

They stand aloof
from all our busy to and fro.
While we rush here and there to sales –
Black Friday, Cyber Monday, Boxing Day –
they hold their peace.

They are the unmoved movers
of our wintering lives,
turning our heads to notice
and our hearts to feel
their concentrated presence.

Like sentinels they stand
to bar the way
to a new season of the spirit
that must await its time.
Then sap will soar
and every bough will bud,
but not yet ...
This is their waiting time.

THE NEWS FROM SIBERIA

The News from Siberia (I)

In the cursed fields of the far north,
where angels fear, the permafrost
is letting loose its huddled hoard,
the demons of the frozen deep,
anthrax and worse, the ancient woes
that haunt the hoary mammoths' sleep.
Hard on their cloven hoofs there goes,
released from ages of restraint,
the murderous murky horde – methane.
Let all the world in every corner weep.

The News from Siberia (II)

Here in the toxic city, built on bones,
closed to the world, the deadbeat bear, displaced
and dazed by hunger, scavenges the dumps
of putrid ready meals and plastic trash
for food that's killing her, while people bring
their kids to stare and snap and share online.
They thought she was a climate refugee
from distant melting ice flows, but perhaps
more likely she was trafficked as a cub,
kept caged for killing for her ice-white pelt.
She is an eminent epitome
of dogged desperation to survive
this world that we have loaded against life.

Note: In June 2019 a starving polar bear was seen roaming the city of Norilsk for several days before being captured and taken to a zoo for medical treatment. Norilsk, built by convicts from the Gulag as a centre for nickel mining and smelting, is one of the most polluted places in the world.

The News from Siberia (III)

Along the sunless shore of Ryrkaypiy,
skirting the sturgid walrus carcasses,
brave Tatyana's Bear Patrol, with sticks
and rubber bullets, keeps the bears at bay.
This year more than usual (seventy-two
some say), hefty as Iorek, lie in wait
for walruses and wheelie bins. They prowl
in temperatures unseasonably high,
irked that the ice will not yet bear their bulk.
The cubs are apt to sidle up the street
and sit on doorsteps like a cuddly toy
Grandfather Frost has left for Christmas fun.
But the intrepid folk of Ryrkaypij
will not evacuate, regardless that
the Institute of Biological
Problems of the North so recommends.
It's time to call our skating party in.
The ice is getting treacherously thin.

Note: *News reports in early December 2019 claimed that the small village of Ryrkaypiy, near the north coast of Chukotka Autonomous Okrug, was overrun by polar bears (exact numbers differed). WWF conservationists claim that the increase in bears prowling around the village, compared with previous years, is due to climate change. Others have suggested that there are more bears because they are doing well, and catching walruses on land is easier than hunting seals on ice. Despite some reports, the bears do not appear to be thin. They are naturally curious animals.*

Iorek Byrnison is the armoured bear in Philip Pullman's His Dark Materials. Grandfather Frost (Ded Moroz) is the Russian version of Santa Claus.

FELLOW CREATURES

Twelve Haiku

Among nameless plants
I remember my mother
remembering their names.

Christopher Smart said
that the true names of flowers
are still in heaven.

Though the trees
may not clap their hands
they dream of it.

Rain clouds again –
still Mount Fuji
eludes me.

Bare to the wind
how gently it sways –
the glade of silver birch.

The gaunt trees of February
branch and point
with such cold clarity.

Ancient trees, afflicted outwardly,
vegetate inward
grow contemplative.

Here among the trees
green
is a whole rainbow of colours.

A single white butterfly
has the whole hot garden
all to itself.

In the morning mist
a squirrel leaping head first
breakfasts upside down.

Gently the mist
wraps up each tree
as a present for God.

In the dear livingness of things
loveliness
and liveliness embrace.

The First Daffodil

I felt its loneliness today –
that single golden daffodil,
daring to broach its life so soon
while thousands keep their comfort still.
Goading the ghosts of winters past,
it whispers winters never last.

The wildest weather of the year
leads nature in a merry dance,
but, partnerless, the daffodil
maintains a solitary stance.
Holding its poise through storm and sun,
its crown of beauty bows to none.

In every springtime, year on year,
nature rehearses for the day
when all will spring to lasting life
and perishing will pass away.
Lonely and luckless though it seem,
the daffodil lives for that dream.

So sometime when I sit alone
and fall into a feckless mood,
I may recall the daffodil,
content to share its solitude.
Like a dear friend who's come to stay,
the daffodil will make my day.

The Heron

The Golden Pavilion, Kyoto, 2016

At dusk, as guidebooks recommend,
tourists mass at Kinkaku-ji.
Its gorgeous gold redoubled in the shimmering lake
is wondrous in all eyes.
But the numinous eludes me.
I blame the groupthink and the selfies
and the vending machines.

Then I see him,
standing apart from it all,
self-contained
in solitary perfect stillness – the heron.
He is the meaning the temple murmurs
in the quiet of the morning
before the crowds encroach.

By Scudamore's Boatyard, Cambridge, 2017

I walk my usual way
beside the meadows into town,
and someone passing says,
'Don't miss the heron – down there to your left!'
He could have said,
'Turn aside to see an apparition!'

The heron stands
in just the same sequestered stillness
intensely himself.
He is the music the meadows make at midnight
for the ears of God alone.

Of course, we know that, biologically,
the motionless wait of a heron
has predatory intent.
But I do not see the swoop of the sharp beak.
I see what cannot be said –
the secret self-identity of otherkind.

The Tree and I

When the tree confronts me
and I turn with expectation,
longing to learn its mystery,
what will the tree say?

Just that it has its own mattering.
Just that it looms and outreaches
regardless of me (though not –
but here I read between the branches –
regardless of God).
Just that its years are not counted
on the same scale as my seventy-two.
Just that it has no interest in
symbolizing anything.
Just that it does speak, volubly even,
but not to me.

And I will look up
at its majestic otherness
and be glad.

Tumbling

The tumbling boughs
of the tall towering pine
pitch towards earth.

Low-flying branches
torn between earth and sky
touch down and upturn.

Half-hidden, high,
behind the uneasy crown,
the sun beams.

It brings to light
between shadows reaches
of radiant green.

Just so the light of God
falls on
our tumbling world.

Angels

They are the beatific boys
as happy as the heavens are high.

They are the galleons of God
that sail the deeps of his desire.

They are the universe's spire
that pierces all of time and space.

They are the hyacinths of heaven
whose fragrance fuels the fires of love.

They are the ancestors of time
who turn the ages into hours.

They are the dancers of the dawn
whose jubilation wakes the sky.

They are the nightingales of noon
whose passion soars above the sun.

They are the standing stones of dusk
that sing the savage world to rest.

They are the panthers of the night
who pace the earth to keep it safe.

They are the midnight messengers
whose wings are wild with songs of peace.

Trees at Christmas

Delving and soaring, the trees get it right,
drawing their being from both earth and sky.
Larches in fall: glory, apricot-bright,
around each slender trunk is floating high,
and high, high up, apricot candyfloss
piles up in mountain miracles of height.
Theirs is the praise that coruscates across
the heavenly ocean into God's delight.

Rootless and skyless stands the Christmas tree,
a different magic, ancient but our own.
Victim of outer dark, it cannot shine
until we dress it like a dryad's shrine.
Our winter praise, our faery liturgy,
dances like fiery sprites before God's throne.

Evening Primrose

While others furl their flowers and droop,
this one with beauty dares the dusk
and woos the soft wings of the night
as hungrily they swerve and swoop.

Its turret of moon-yellow blooms
beams the clear fragrance of its life
into the dark, while flesh and blood
lie half alive in dreamy rooms.

When all the rest awake reborn,
it joins their nodding to the sun,
treasuring its secret life alone.
It is the flower that wakes the dawn.

Note: For the last line, see Psalm 57.8.

The Grey Heron

For Brother Herbert

She lives by stillness and intensity.
Nothing eludes her high and haughty gaze.
Unmoving and unmoved, but poised to pounce,
she is the queen of all that she surveys.

Here in her cloudless patch of paradise,
aloof from troubles outside her domain,
she is the emblem of another world
where wonder and serenity would reign.

Black Holes

Once there were sky dragons,
born of blind rage.
Sometimes one of them,
rampaging across the firmament,
would swallow the sun.

Now we have black holes,
infinities of nothing.
Passionless they lurk.
Some day one of them
will swallow the galaxy.

POEMS OF THE PANDEMIC

Virus

Like some malign magician it has cast
a curse that turns all closeness, every touch
into a poisoned cup we dare not share.
It locks all sacramental dealings down.

Self-distancing is this year's Lenten fast.
God only knows how long this Lent will last.

When the sworn enemy of incarnate love
confronted Jesus in the wilderness,
his magic met its match. The always close
companion of the lonesome stood steadfast.

Back to the Future

I walked on ancient tracks today,
through leafy lanes where centuries
of feet have trodden down their way
to toil in fields or, freed from work,
to worship on their high Lord's Day.

It wasn't that I'd found a crack
in time through which I could recede,
but time itself, with time to spare
in this quiescent world, had rolled
the accelerating ages back.

Beside the brook, along the baulk,
before enclosures tore the times
and furrowed shares in common fields
were old as churchyards, in the steps
of shorter, slower lives I walk.

True, these are tricks of lockdown time.
The lusty birds and murmuring trees
seem timeless, but the larks are gone
for ever, and the distant din
of the remorseless motorway goes on.

Yet (for I hear it whispered on the breeze)
a journey back could be a journey on.

At Christmas in a Pandemic

I want to see the sun dance.
I want to see its party gown,
its cheeky smile, its paper crown.
I want to see it bounce
on the horizon like a ball of fire.
I want to see it spin with joy
and spark the world's delight.
So everywhere that sadness seeps
into a home like damp,
I want to see it light a lamp
of gladness burning bright.

I want to hear the moon sing.
I want to hear her carolling,
her pure voice as it waxes
from crescent to crescendo.
I want to see it touch the hearts
of all the lonely, all the lost,
the grieved beyond consoling.
I want to hear a blue moon croon
the blues till a new song is born.
Then all the stars of every night
will orchestrate the dawn.

I want a star to follow
through this bewildered world.
I want to see it leap from heaven,
its meteoric eagerness
to be the leading light
in this most epic journey of the heart.
I want to see the wonder of the wise,
those scryers of the skies,
the dawning expectation in their eyes.
I want the star to lead
beyond the limits of our learning
finally into sight.

Living with Covid

(They say we must learn to live with the virus.)

Like an unwanted guest, it snoops around,
sniffing in cupboards, fingering the dirt
you left undusted, snoozes in your chair,
and when your friends drop by it's always there.

It used to be a hydra-headed foe
we grappled, armed with sanitizing gel,
until, over the hill, the cavalry,
Boris's boffins, rode to jab us free.

But VV (Victory over Virus) Day
is not on the horizon now, they say.
Cowed but still smirking, much like death itself,
this cuckoo in your nest is here to stay.

THE CHURCH YEAR

Advent

Haiku for an Advent Calendar

Day 1 – Genesis
After paradise
not even Lot's wife looks
   back.
Memory turns round.

Day 2 – Exodus
The bones of Joseph
in their gilt sarcophagus
travel night and day.

Day 3 – Leviticus
If she is too poor
to afford a sheep, she may
offer two pigeons.

Day 4 – Numbers
Dawn in my distance,
the wise watchers will see
   him,
star of their searching.

Day 5 – Deuteronomy
Moses from Pisgah
overviews all. It is not
space but time he lacks.

Day 6 – Joshua
Going over Jordan
Joshua above all sees
that the ark goes first.

Day 7 – Judges
Said the trees to the
bramble, 'Come, be our ruler!'
'Wait!' said the mustard.

Day 8 – Samuel
Hannah, drunk as an
apostle at Pentecost,
magnifies the Lord.

Day 9 – Kings
She came with riddles.
His more than answers more
   than
took her breath away.

Day 10 – Isaiah
In the wilderness
a voice cries for centuries
seeking an echo.

Day 11 – *Jeremiah*
Rachel refuses
to be comforted – even
when we turn the page.

Day 12 – *Ezekiel*
In the end it is
all in the name of the city:
The Lord is there.

Day 13 – *The Twelve
    Prophets*
Then, as before, will
Bethlehem bear the shepherd
of the scattered sheep.

Day 14 – *Psalms*
If there were glory
only, praise like the last
psalms,
would that be the end?

Day 15 – *Proverbs*
Too clever by half
are the foolish. The wise
    know
the folly of God.

Day 16 – *Job*
God answered Job but
not his question. Maybe he
will do that again.

Day 17 – *Song of Solomon*
Yes, he will haste like
a gazelle. Nothing is more
impatient than love.

Day 18 – *Ruth*
Tough old Naomi
bounces a child on her knee –
her wild hope come home.

Day 19 – *Lamentations*
Jerusalem hurls
her desperate hopes against
God's forgetfulness.

Day 20 – *Ecclesiastes*
Whatever God does
and whoever else may be
who knows? The wise wait.

Day 21 – *Esther*
Probability
counts for nothing when
Esther's
G-d is in the plot.

Day 22 – *Daniel*
Nebuchadnezzar
dreams of the doom of despots
and the wide world wakes.

Day 23 – *Ezra-Nehemiah*
After the exile
returnees do not look back
more than can be helped.

Day 24 – *Chronicles*
Adam, Seth, Enoch,
Noah, Abraham, David,
Zerubbabel ...

Note: The sequence is that of the 24 books of the Hebrew Bible.

Advent

We long for glory.

Sometimes,
when horrors haunt us –
the bombed hospitals,
the children raped and silenced,
the endless histories of hate –
when horror haunts our undistracted moments,
only the longing
softens our hard hearts
and fires concern.

We long for glory,
scarcely knowing what it is.
We long for that supernal dawn to break
wherever there is keening for the loved and lost,
ending the world's wake.
We long to greet that rising sun
whose rays will melt
the tanks, the torture chambers
and the iron fists
of evil's mighty show.
We long for light
to flood the streets where lust and lies
lurk in the shadows to entice their prey.

Evolution designed us, it seems,
as optimistic animals.
Positive thinking was advantageous.
But longing stirs
way beyond optimism.
It strains to see
not the bright side of life
but glory.

Amid the rubble of the doomed cities
children play,
defying bombs and mortars –
a make-believe that may perhaps come true
when truth becomes
the one who makes it true
and we believe.

He is the man of sorrows –
of all the sorrows of all times
and of this sorry earth.
There is no face like his
where truth and beauty,
passion and compassion
meld into glory.

We long to see his glory.

Dies Irae

Come, Lion of Judah! Rage and roar
above our mad self-deafening din!

Come, Torch of Liberty, and shine
in every nook of every heart!

Come, Stone of Destiny, and smash
the grinning idols of our greed!

Come, Hound of Heaven, and hunt down
the fetid foe in his dark hide!

Come, Ring of Power, to rule them all!
Perfect your reign of peace and joy!

Come soon, Great Wave, and sluice the stench
of evil from this sullied earth!

Come, Ancient Wizard! Wave your wand!
Turn our stale waters into wine!

Come soon, Green Man! Re-wild these wastes!
Unfurl your foliage far and wide!

Come, Wounded Healer! Pour your salve
on ravaged lives and savaged minds!

Come, Rising Sun, and raise us from
our graves to greet the new day's dawn.

Come, Wind of Change! Blow through your world
and fill dead lungs with power to praise!

Come soon, Blood Brother, to your kin
who pine from lonely lack of you!

Come, Alpha and Omega! Write
the story's happy-ever-after end!

Christmas

First Light

After all the false dawns,
who is this who unerringly paints
the first rays in their true colours?
We have kept vigil with owls
when the occult noises of the night
fell tauntingly silent
and a breeze got up
as if for morning.
This time the trees tremble.
Is it with a kind of reckless joy
at the gentle light
lapping their leaves
like the very first turn of a tide?
Timid creatures creep out of burrows
sensing kindness
and the old crow on the cattle-shed roof
folds his wings and dreams.

Song of the Shepherds

We were familiar with the night.
We knew its favourite colours,
its sullen silence
and its small, disturbing sounds,
its unprovoked rages,
its savage dreams.

We slept by turns,
attentive to the flock.
We said little.
Night after night, there was little to say.
But sometimes one of us,
skilled in that way,
would pipe a tune of how things were for us.

They say that once, almost before time,
the stars with shining voices
serenaded
the newborn world.
The night could not contain their boundless praise.

We thought that just a poem –
until the night
a song of solar glory,
unutterable, unearthly,
eclipsed the luminaries of the night,
as though the world were exorcised of dark
and, coming to itself, began again.

Later we returned to the flock.
The night was ominously black.
The stars were silent as the sheep.
Nights pass, year on year.
We clutch our meagre cloaks against the cold.
Our aging piper's fumbling fingers play,
night after night,
an earthly echo of the song that banished dark.
It has stayed with us.

The Christmas Story

Here begins (although it is possible
to start before the beginning)
the story of all our stories.

If we step in out of the night
they are there before us.
Among the huge gentle standing shapes of animals
it is the human group that seems sheltered.
They are enclosed in that still moment
angelic presences await.
But soon they too will be fugitives
on the way that lies open before us.

If we were to pause long enough
in the lost moment that glimmers,
that one night before our dark nights,
long enough to see
the primal sympathy,
the high humility
and – for this before all is before us –
the giftedness of all that matters most
seen in the glad bestowal of God's self,

then we should perhaps look up again
in recognition when our paths cross –
at a brother's too early grave,
in a beggar's shuffle towards us,
seeing the crows scavenge,
when there are places of honour to be filled,
as the night falls without comfort.

This story has not ended (although
it is possible to begin again). Telling it
leaves our own stories unfinished.

The bleary Cows

Nativity scenes grow rarer by the year,
like snow, and in the wake of godliness
the trolls return – with neolithic fear
not quite disguised by grinning ugliness.

We miss the question and the cosmic yes,
the oddly reverent goat and the shy goose,
the high and haloed ones, the gentleness
of heaven with earth in Giotto's lights and hues.

But still they come, the partridges and pears,
the penguins, pokemons and polar bears,
the tartan reindeer and old mother time.

And like the audience at the pantomime,
'Oh yes he did!' we yell, 'Look – in the sight
of bleary cows – he came and there was light.'

The Adoration

They are all there as ever, but are we?
They are so fully there. Even the ox,
as present as the moment, bides all time.
They are the master-key to all deadlocks,
the endlessly inflected paradigm
of all our making sense and letting be.

The star is still, the camels rest, and there
are those who journeyed from its birth to his
in search of being. Here they have arrived.
They are the whither that shall be and is,
when all our yesteryears have been revived
and all our wanderings are otherwhere.

The mother holds the eternal to herself,
embracing her presentiment of loss,
wholly herself in being there for him.
They are the river we may never cross,
in which we must for ever sink or swim,
fleeing or finding the self-sundered self.

Dayspring from on High

Whether there are also births that raise
no hopes, whose still surfaces reflect no glint
of sunlight into a mother's opaque stare,
hinges on which doors slam shut,
as there were also births that gleamed
under the cold lustre of Herod's swords,
we can perhaps endure to ask
on the long walk home from Bethlehem.

Approaching Christmas through the Mist

The world is blurred.
The mind's clear grasp is loosed.
Familiarity is lost,
faded in mist.

The wintering trees
have softer silhouettes
that manifest
a gentler grace.

Mist is not fog.
We do not lose the way
but find it changed,
less well defined.

The little town,
waking in dreamy haze,
awaits us still,
pregnant with peace.

All hopes and fears,
clouded or clearly cut,
meet again here.
Love is undimmed.

Canticles for the Twelve Days of Christmas

1 Partridge perching,
  you assure us
  of True Love's
  self-giving for us.

2 The time has arrived for
  our God to be manned,
  and the voice of the turtle
  is heard in our land.

3 French hens, spread
  your wings around him.
  Herod's henchmen
  haste to hound him.

4 Calling birds,
  your calls revise!
  Salute the
  bird of paradise!

5 The age of gold
  comes into view!
  Ring out the old!
  Ring in the new!

6 Geese a-laying,
  take a gander
  at this child
  laid in a manger!

7 Swans a-swimming,
  know before long
  he must also
  sing his swansong!

8 Maids a-milking,
  marvel at
  the mother-maid's
  Magnificat!

9 Ladies dancing,
  tread your measure!
  Celebrate
  God's hidden treasure!

10 Leaping lords,
  your Lord address,
  who leapt from heaven
  to lowliness!

11 Pipers piping,
  lead us longing
  to the heart
  of all belonging!

12 Drummers, keep your
  drumbeats beating!
  Evil's armies
  are retreating.

Epiphany

The Journey of the Magi

Into the terrible distance of the stars
habitually they gazed
gaunt from the journeys of so many nights
spent on the borderlands of the mind's range.

But of this new distance
into whose crossing the self steps
down they had no map. There was no gauging it
even when the goal drew near

and they who had built themselves
like tall houses into the sky
stooped where the heavens bent
towards the squat stable.

The Magi tell of their Journey

It was an immense desolation we travelled –
through derelict and stale spaces,
along streets of abandoned settlements
where lost souls jeered at us
among the bombed and burned tenements,
below caves and crevices
where bitter devisers of vengeance hid out,
across poisoned deserts
and land-mined landscapes of death,
place after destitute place.

How much further have we to go?

We did what the star did,
knowing nothing else.
It was small light to go by.
Sometimes others shared our way –
fugitives and forgotten ones,
traumatized children clutching our hearts,
wild camels and hunted creatures,
strange pilgrims shouting abuse at heaven,
and one sleepwalker wandering blindly in the world's night.
We could only go where the star went,
and some called us fools,
but it was the only wisdom we had.

How much further have we to go?

There was another shack in a dirt lane.
Accustomed courtiers
we knew well enough the hyperboles of power,
the calculated benefactions of the great,
the starry destinies of empire.
But our paeans of proud deference failed.
We could make no account
of this new constellation.
As for our tribute
it was less gift than surrender.

   How much further have we to go?

The Star

We first saw it
on a night pitch as a dungeon,
the world's midnight.
It appeared
the only brightness in the universe,
a bird of pure light soaring,
a crystal ship
sailing the dark deluge,
a dazzling denizen of heaven
leaping the vast vault
towards our long-lost world.

And so we scrolled through
the pages of our predecessors,
sages and soothsayers,
far-sighted seekers of signs.
We pondered prophecies
penned at twilight
when the mind scries unicorns
and ghouls lurking in trees
and doubts its destiny.

And it seemed to us for the first time
that they knew nothing
save the yearning
for the blue flower
in a starlit clearing
among moon-white trees.

Into our calendar of moons
and slow rotations
the star was a wild intruder
routing regularities.
At the world's midnight it arose,
morning star of an incalculable day,
whose hours we could not reckon.

From our high hermitages,
from their wide vistas and airy aspirations,
we descended through forests,
finding a path we had never travelled,
though it felt familiar,
like the last leg of a journey home.

But there were many legs
and lengths we had to go to,
led as we were.

We moved like shadows
seeking the selves that cast them
in the light that defines them.

There were desolate spaces
where even the camels stood
snorting at unseen evil.

We skirted murderous towns
where the rotting dead
hung in avenues of gallows.

We met the mad king,
heard his cunning words of welcome,
saw the desperation in his eyes.

In the end we arrived
where a sturdy man stood guard,
like a silver-armoured angel,
and the mother of all meaning,
girl though she was,
glowed with the love
that leapt lightly from heaven.
Here was the home for all strangers.
Here was the world's dawn.
Here was the blue flower
in the sunlit clearing
among milk-white trees.

The Magi return to their own Country by another Way

They at least – the austere ones,
the gurus with the abstracted eyes,
on the one unrepeatable journey –

They at least – the heaven staring –
the intent traversers of night,
on the journey into particularity –

They at least – the wonderers,
the significant faces
prone and denoted on the stable floor –

They at least for all their ancient wisdom
did not betray him.

The Magi remember

This year they feel so far – as if we stood
still by a parapet in the blank night
waiting for stars, bearing the sky's sad weight
as trodden earth bears down upon the dead.

This year they hide from us – as on the night
mothers beyond consoling took their place
in dreams from which we fled directionless,
afraid to ask our star-forsaken route.

This year the darkness cradles him again,
shadows his parents, shelters their escape.
Far from us travels our and all our hope,
the morning star of our still-distant dawn.

'He took the child and his mother by night'

(Matthew 2.14)

This year we have seen them so often,
trudging, intrepid,
one clutching a child
to whom the other's eyes
at every second step
return, solicitous, alert,
fighting fatigue
for him, their treasured trust.

Week after week we watch
the trudging millions,
dauntless, unstoppable.
Through fire and water they have come,
desperate for hope.
They would walk continents,
batter the gates of every fabled city,
dodge boiling oil and scale the battlements,
shouting, 'We too are human!'

Less visible to us
but constant in the tearful gaze of God,
lambs are led to slaughter,
nasrani to the last,
leaves of the lustrous trees of paradise
falling, golden,
into his open arms,
his trusty treasure.

Candlemas

Wait and see
(Simeon and Anna)

In the drab waiting room
the failed travellers, resigned, sleep
on the hard benches, inured
to postponement and foul coffee.
Hope has given up on them.

There are also the impatient,
pacing platforms, and the driven,
purple with frustration, abusing
their mobiles, for the hardest part
of waiting is the not doing.

Truly to wait is pure dependence.
But waiting too long the heart
grows sclerotic. Will it still
be fit to leap when the time comes?
Prayer is waiting with desire.

Two aged lives incarnate
century on century
of waiting for God, their waiting room
his temple, waiting on his presence,
marking time by practising

the cycle of the sacrifices,
ferial and festival,
circling onward, spiralling
towards a centre out ahead,
seasons of revolving hope.

Holding out for God who cannot
be given up for dead, holding
him to his promises – not now,
not just yet, but soon, surely,
eyes will see what hearts await.

Ash Wednesday

Ash Wednesday

This smudge of ash brands us like Cain,
who wore his guilt for all to see,
the murderer condemned to live.
He built a city, spawned a tribe
and watched a whole world wax and wane.

Somewhere back there we lost the plot –
fleeing or seeking, we no longer knew,
for east of Eden every road
leads back to self. No self-love or
self-harm can blot out Cain's damned spot.

This cross-mark indicates a man,
the innocent condemned to die,
who, when the cries of all the wronged,
slaughtered like Abel, filled the skies,
did what none but the source of all love can.

He broke the entail of our guilt,
the guilt we own and guilt we share,
and pioneered the pilgrim way,
out of the city named for self,
along the high road hope has built.

Now he has left his mark on us,
the hallmark of his handiwork.
There can be now no turning back
along the angry streets that wind
to where they nailed him with the murderous.

*Note: The poem refers to the custom of placing ashes in the shape of a
cross on the foreheads of worshippers in churches, on Ash Wednesday,
the first day of Lent.*

Good Friday

Darkness at Noon

To see the love here in its labours lost
our eyes must grow accustomed to the dark.
They see it best who sorrow at his side,
the mother and the friend who loved him most.

They see his harrowed flesh, the blood, the dirt.
They feel the pangs that wrench him from the wood
and hurl him back, torn, tethered by the nails.
They hear his silent thirsting for his God.

The darkness darker than the dread of death
descends as though God de-created light.
He enters our despairing need of God,
the twisted traumas of our loss of faith.

The darkness bears down on him like the weight
of all the sorrows of this blighted earth.
Compassion throbs through all his weary pain.
His love grows strongest as his powers abate.

So with the love that lightens all, he blessed
his mother and the friend he loved the best.

Phoenix

Bird of the paradise of our desires,
I hear your joy in all the fragrant woods,
and in the crimson glory of your wings
I glimpse the dream that lures you to your pyre.

You are the one and only of your kind –
No mate, no chicks, no selfish DNA.
You do not strut your beauty to impress.
Like beauty's self you live to play and pray.

You are the fable that has fanned our flames
of mortal longing for eternity.
When aeons wane we scan the eastern skies
and yearn for some pristine identity.

Our Phoenix! From the paradise of God
earthward on wings of ardent love you flew
and gave yourself to hell's consuming blaze
once and for all to make our worn world new.

Easter

Four Women and a Tomb

After so much slow sorrow,
emptied of feeling,
drained dry of hope,
still their love led them.

At the third cockcrow
on the third morning
they gathered,
heads cloaked and baskets
weighty with fragrance.

Out of love's fullness
he poured himself, emptied,
an offering,
sweet-scented as April
in the garden of God.

That spring of all loving
that never runs dry
poured a deep draught for them,
quenching their emptiness
– an emptied tomb
and wonder, heart-whelming wonder.

Easter Reverie

The willows lead the leafing of the trees.
The meadows are exuberantly green.
Like fireflies dancing, sunshine shimmers on
the ripples of the river. Rapturous birds
invite the world to share their heavenly joy.

I know this place so well – its silent swans,
its congregating cows – and yet, today,
it seems to me so fresh it might have come
straight from the heart and hands of God's desire,
reflecting still the sunlight of his face.

This Eden knows mortality. A tree,
felled by the storms, lies a majestic wreck.
Yet from its mighty trunk new branches rise
like spires to heaven. 'There is hope for a tree.'
Elated in the balmy air I dream.

Can there be life so truly new
that death itself is dying out?

Note: The quotation is from Job 14.7 (and the context is relevant).

Early April Flowers

This is the season of the lowly flowers,
with names evoking long-forgotten times:
the primrose and the lesser celandine,
the cowslip, daisy and forget-me-not.
They lay their bounteous beauty at our feet.
We could, were we so minded, stamp on them.
Instead they stir our hearts with thanks to God
who came to us in human lowliness.
They stamped on him; they stamped him out; and yet,
like spring itself, he blossoms all the more.

Pentecost

A Pentecost Prayer to the Spirit of Life

Fountain of life,
wash our worn feet,
weary from sleepwalking.
We have stumbled
through the deluded dead of night,
lost in a maze of desire,
enticed by tall tales
of travellers who fell famished
on the lost path to the fabled goal.

Fountain of life,
slake our parched spirits.
We have snaked
through the arid sands of today
in search of tomorrow.
We have survived the sun scorching
and the moon menacing
and the spells of the desert demons,
tracking the mirage.

Fountain of life,
cool our fevered foreheads,
marked with the fateful lineage of Cain.
Finally we find you,
source of all searching,
soul friend for the journey,
guide to all changing landscapes of living.
Work your white magic,
fill us with your future,
wellspring of ever-new torrents of life.

ODES TO FRANCIS OF ASSISI

Il Poverello

She was your true love – Lady Poverty.
In that springtime of your vocation,
amid the almond blossom, virgin white,
you wooed her and pursued her.

With eager joy you undertook
the trials of your love. They were both pain
and poetry. Her troubadour,
you made your life a chanson in her praise.

Romance aside, it was your Lord you loved,
his poverty and passion you embraced.
With him you slept in haylofts, tramped barefoot
and kissed his love, the leper, on the lips.

Like him you took the lowest place,
where you could not humiliate the poor
or patronize. Penniless on principle,
you had good news – only good news – to share.

You sought the clarity of being poor,
clear as the stream on Mount Subasio,
where in the caves you slept on beds of stone
and rose enraptured by the songs of dawn.

You longed to count for nothing,
stripped of the things that we invest
our self-worth and our self-importance in,
so that for you God could be everything.

So poverty became extravagance,
free of all niggardly restraint,
generous as Brother Sun,
wide as the arms of Christ.

The Cross at San Damiano

You were drawn to small, neglected churches
just as you were to lepers and the poor.
God met you in the lowliest of places
and hid in a small task your greater call.

Your sense of God was sensory. You saw
and touched this dusty icon, heard this Christ
who, crucified, no longer hangs but stands,
wide-eyed and radiant, wondrously alive.

His eyes, serene and steadfast, fix their gaze
upon his Father. In that interchange
of loving sight all creatures are in view.
His wounds attest his love, his arms invite.

Below his feet are figures now obscured
by hundreds who, like you, have touched and kissed.
Among those obscure faces was your own,
gazing and weeping, waiting for a word.

Note: This poem is about the occasion when Francis, praying in front of the icon of the crucified Christ in the little church of San Damiano, heard the words: 'Repair my church.' His immediate response was to repair the crumbling building he was in. The icon can be seen at https:// en.wikipedia.org/wiki/San_Damiano_cross#/media/File:Kruis_san_ damiano.gif (accessed 17.2.22) and elsewhere online.

A Song for Brother Sun

He was your liege lord – Brother Sun.
Daily you paid court as he rode
in majesty across the high heaven,
shining his favours on fair Umbria.

Daily from Brother Sun the glory poured,
filling your heart with penitence and praise.
Praise was your suntrap where you bared your soul
and in his borrowed glory gladly basked.

Borrowed it was, kindled each day anew,
the truest image of the world's true light,
just as your praise, kindled by Brother Sun,
glowed with the glory of the Most High God.

Praise was your metier, your paradise,
your liberation from the bonds of self,
the ecstasy you shared with crickets, birds
and every sibling of bright Brother Sun.

Note: This poem was inspired by The Canticle of the Creature, *also known as* The Canticle of Brother Sun.

A Song for Sister Moon

She was your sole companion – Sister Moon
– those nights you passed in prayer on mountainsides.
She drew close to you, while the stars remained,
though sisters too, a universe away.

You loved the silver-white humility
with which she rules the night, the tenderness
with which she lets the tired world rest. You were
two solitary saints in love with God.

Did she remind you of your Sister Clare?
Did you in spirit see her convent bathed
in Sister Full Moon's cool and tranquil light?
Maybe your moonlit prayers communed with hers.

You felt for Sister Moon as, month by month,
she followed Jesus' way of waning and
of self-eclipse that you must follow too.
She was your soul friend in your soul's dark night.

Note: *This poem was inspired by* The Canticle of the Creatures, *also known as* The Canticle of Brother Sun.

A Song for Brother Fire

He was your best mate – Brother Fire.
A cheeky chappie, he could cheer you up.
At murky dusk his laughter crackled like
the light that darkness never can defeat.

You marvelled at the magic of his mirth,
transforming inert logs to leaping flames
and dancing lights. Just so a spark of love
enflames the dull heart with desire for God.

You loved his swaggering vigour. Even when
he burned a bothy to the ground, you were
indulgent, reverent even, would not let
them quench the ardour of your Brother Fire.

But did you recognize his shifting shape
that night of all-transcending pain and joy
when as the seraph, heavenly prince of fire,
he burned the marks of love into your flesh?

Note: *This poem was inspired by* The Canticle of the Creatures, *also
known as* The Canticle of Brother Sun.

A Song for the Most High

After the vision and the searing pain –
praises. Heart brimming over, spirit blazing,
hands held in homage, side bloody with praise.
Praise is all your being burns to be.

You felt immersed in goodness – goodness of the One
who alone is good, *the* Good, source of all good,
source of the glory coursing through your veins,
source of the passion piercing to the marrow.

So your praise ponders all that God is for us:
patience and hope, humility and wisdom,
beauty, refreshment, justice, joy and love –
all that is honey to the taste of praise.

He is the Most High, higher than a mind
can think or heart imagine. Yet he is
also with us, abject as a man
who sweats blood in an olive grove for us.

Note: This poem is inspired by The Praises of God, *which Francis composed after receiving the stigmata.*

A Song for Sister Death

She had not always seemed your sister – Death.
Not when she butchered your comrades-in-arms,
or when, a harridan with bloody hands,
she terrorized your post-traumatic dreams.

But now, a lifetime later, you and she
are reconciled. Now, like a patient friend,
she waits to open wide for you the door
to all life's loveliness redeemed and more.

You cannot fear her now that you have lived
the dying of your Lord in your own flesh.
His dying love has made peace with your foe.
His living love will never let you go.

Each day the brothers sing your song of joy
for all the creatures you no longer see,
and at the end you lie on Mother Earth
while Songbird Sisters celebrate your birth.

Note: This poem was inspired by The Canticle of the Creatures, *also
known as* The Canticle of Brother Sun.

*By the time he wrote it Francis was going blind. When he was dying he
asked to be laid on the earth naked as he was when he was born.*

TALES OF THE EAST NEUK

The Isle of May

Prayers gathered round it like the seals
that croon their soulful songs at dusk,
and men who fished for drowning folk
rowed with redemption in their creels.

Nightly in solitary cells
they drove the demons to their doom,
then slept in paradisal peace,
secure from fiendish spooks and spells.

Elijah-like on the lone isle,
their faith was fed by birds from God.
Each morning on the rocks their feet
were washed by waves that he had trod.

In winter when the days were dark
and storms blew high around the isle,
Fifers in shuttered homes would hear
praises resounding from the ark.

Note: *In the ninth century, there was a monastic community, established by St Adrian, on the Isle of May (off the coast of Fife, in the Firth of Forth). It was brought to an end by Viking raids, in which Adrian and many of the monks were massacred, but monks again lived on the island in the twelfth and thirteenth centuries. Needless to say, this poem is entirely imaginary, but, if it is to be placed chronologically, it would more appropriately relate to the first community on the island.*

The Blue Stane of Crail

Astride the isle the devil took aim.
His brows were grim, his smile irate.
The God-devoted folk of Crail
had roused his heart of boundless hate.

A plague had rampaged through the town.
The monster clawed at every door.
But all who could still laboured hard
to salve the sick and feed the poor.

The plague abated. But, as soon
as fishermen returned to work,
blond raiders came across the sea.
They burned the boats and robbed the kirk.

Still people knelt before a cross
and filled despondent hands with tears,
an offering to the God who gave
sadly his Son to share their loss.

The devil danced atop the May.
He hurled the boulder of his wrath.
It split in two and missed its mark.
It often does when good folk pray.

*Note: Near the church gates in Crail there is an erratic boulder known
as the Blue Stane (stone). The story is that the devil, on the Isle of May,
threw a large rock at the kirk. It split in the air, one piece landing close
to the kirk, but missing it, the other piece landing on the shore at nearby
Balcomie. Everything else in this poem is imaginary.*

The Hermit and the King
(Constantine's Cave)

Here at the extremity of the east,
where sky and sea aim to be all,
the man of God aspired to be
God's lowly one, least of the least.

Standing in waves of heavenly blue,
he loved to lose himself in God
and, with the turning of the tide,
receive himself from God anew.

With praises he was never done.
Cicadas joined his song at noon.
Vespers he sang with seals and told
his rosary with the rising sun.

Some nights he heard the deathly noise
of spectral clashes on the plain,
the clang of swords on jagged rocks,
the battle songs of Pict and Dane.

On sabbath days he preached the word
to fulmars, gulls and guillemots.
He gave God's bread to all God's own
of every tribe of beast and bird.

He watched the dark ships of the foe.
He could not curse, could only bless,
and so he lit the warning fires
high on the summit of the Ness.

The days were holy when the haar
rolled in and all but blinded him,
for clouded so the Glory came
riding upon the cherubim.

A lonely phantom of the fight,
King Constantine, the Song of Scots,
came bloodied to the cave one night:
'Grant me, good friend, a shriven end.'

He knelt beside the lowly one
and prayed till they could pray no more.
A battleaxe beheaded both –
the man of peace, the man of war.

*Historical note: Constantine I, king of the Picts and Scots, was called
'Song of the Scots' (Duan Albanach) because of his heroism. He died
in a battle with the Danes in 874 or 876. He was deserted on the field
of battle by most of his army and killed by the Danes. It is not certain
where in Fife the battle took place, but local tradition associates it with
the Black Cave on Balcomie Sands, close to Fife Ness, now known as
'Constantine's Cave'. The hermit is entirely my own invention, but there
is evidence of Christian habitation of the cave at some time(s).*

Saint Fillan

Scent of wild roses and the tang of sea,
salted with seaweed, stayed with him all night,
coloured his dreams, pervaded every hour
he waited on the Lord of all delight.

He laboured by the supernatural light
that spilled from his own arm upon the page.
What once had been a wound that would not heal
burned bright like seraphim in holy rage.

Painstakingly he copied every line,
all his devotion poured into his art.
He felt illuminated like a book
and saw each word inscribed upon his heart.

Strange beasts unwound themselves around his text
and peered into the radiant eyes of seers
whose mouths disgorged their prophecies in strips.
Small gaping rabbits raised attentive ears.

In other margins faces would appear
of those the Word himself came to redeem.
He drew them all from life, for well he knew
the godless fisherfolk of Pittenweem.

Leaving his ink to dry, he left the cave
to walk the shore and taste the zesty spray.
He loved the scurvy-grass and gillyflowers.
Like incense they incited him to pray

*Note: The Celtic saint Fillan of Pittenweem lived as a recluse in a cave,
which can be visited. He is said to have spent his time copying manu-
scripts of the sacred texts. To enable him to do so without the lavish
expense of candles, his left arm was miraculously made to glow. Though
he is commonly identified with the more famous St Fillan who came
from Ireland and lived in other parts of Scotland in the seventh century,
it seems uncertain whether he was the same man.*

SEASONS

Five Haiku

Will the shadow on
the sundial turn back? Will the
autumn shades turn green?

The last snowdrops –
just when we were moving on
to higher things.

My Christmas cactus,
as though it lived before Christ,
blooms in October.

Over my shoulder
I see the backs of the years
evading me still.

Golden leaves we are –
the high wind of the Spirit
blows us all away.

Premature Spring

Spirit of bursting blossom,
rose-tinted white,
lightsome as birdsong,
uplift our surprise
on your soft soaring wings,
up, up to the Lord of delight.

Spring at last!

Open at last the shutters.
Breathe the delight.
Watch the clouds sail their limitless blue.
This is faith.

Hawthorn blossom –
white fire igniting
hope for high summer,
when the bright sun of heaven
will warm
our hearts to brimming.

The woods barely
begin to green.
Still we can gaze
through endless avenues
that soon will fill
with colours soft and shady,
like the love that buds,
unfurls and fills our future.

Dazzled

Now the daydreams of summer
must endure
the clarity of autumn.

The sun hangs low
and targets probing glares
at every leaf
trembling to fall.

On faces upturned to it,
grateful, smiling,
it is slow to warm
but quick to dazzle.

Murky and misanthropic
seem the days
the sun fails to show.

Shorter and paler are the others,
as the leaves lapse
and fade to dust.

But still there is no rush
to say to winter,
'Bring it on. We are ready.'

Still in the pools of sunshine,
cool and clear,
we may observe ourselves

muddied and murky,
frail as crumbling leaves
but even now in dwindling days
sunstruck,
dazzling as we are dazzled.

Travelling on

For the journey I pack
well-travelled trust
insoles for old feet and old souls
some practice on the track
and an expectant heart.

Deep in the flame-birch wood
the trees grow drowsy.
Uncharted ways
bewitch
all to the good.

At Terminal 2
the talk is of flight.
We are all migrants now,
we survivors,
fleeing the tyranny of the new.

Main Street.
Small town.
Passing through.
Front porch.
Local brew.
Here they live complacently and neat
or so it seems.
Travelling on.

Autumnal winds,
have your wild way with us.
In your armfuls of glory
gather us too.
Break our fall.
Blow our minds.

At the extreme of our lives,
could we but find it,
an overgrown path
peters unexpectedly
out on the windswept outcrop
where an old boathouse
survives.

Elegy

Although the trees catch fire or rust,
this fall it is the murk that wraps
my spirit in its mourning wear
and whispers: All must come to dust.

Yet sometimes in a musty wood
a poem proves an old white witch
who with her wand of words transmutes
the brown leaves to a golden mood.

Though every wanwood must unleave
and every heart grieve in the dust,
there is a word so maple-red
it turns autumnal shades to trust.

'All must come to dust' is quoted from the song in Shakespeare's Cym-
beline, *and lines 9–10 (including the word 'wanwood') allude to Gerard
Manley Hopkins' poem 'Spring and Fall' (better known by its first line:
'Margaret, are you grieving').*

THE SEA, THE SEA!

Five Haiku

The lonely posts
of old breakwaters –
a beach where no one goes

Cloud hangs
only over this bay
with its jagged black rocks

Where the great wave struck
only the wreck of the disaster-prevention centre
remains

This also is praise:
seals on a sandbank at dusk
wailing their weird hymn

To listen only
to the waves, not to my mind –
would be blissful

The Path to the Sea

It would be well-trodden gravel
turning sandy near the seaward end,
fringed by a scattering of poppies
or valerian or seaside daisies,
hedged by gorse bushes or brambles
and a low weathered wall.

Do I remember it?
It has the tugging power of deep nostalgia.
There is a path I often took in recent years
that felt to be a reminiscence
of one much further back.
I cannot tell.

Memory or not,
this picture leads me by the hand
down to a quiet beach.
I'd like to hire a blue beach hut
and in my dotage doze,
lulled by the lisping motion of the waves,
and regress to those distant days
when such a path led to a sea of dreams.

To Matthew Arnold

There is no sadness in the sea,
only in your disillusioned gaze,
waking from dreams
with that frail haunting sense
of something lovely lost beyond recall.

You hear an absence in the tidal roll.
I hear a presence,
insistent, reassuringly sustained.
The absence I detect is in the urban din.

God is the endless ocean.
From its depths waves wash
the naked shingles of our world.
They press their presence on the shifting strand,
shoring the fringe where sea gives place to land.
Ebbing they leave their shimmer on the sand.
Sometimes they surge and storm and pound,
sometimes they lap.

The tide recedes far out,
but it will turn, softly at first,
no doubt.

This poem responds to Matthew Arnold's poem 'On Dover Beach'.

To Gerard Manley Hopkins

For the stressed-out soul what more soothing salve
than this: to moor the mind to a green shore,
to let it float sun-splattered on the spangled blue
and gently with the serried ripples rise and fall?

Still the sound of tide's fall and flow,
pure and timeless, as it pleased your ear, survives,
but its twin voice, the lark's, has died away
with time, unhoused by our gross grandizement.

Is nature ever spent? Since you remoulded words
to trace the inscape of each God-beloved thing,
man's tread has trodden dead the springs of life
and sullied to its roots the age-long growth God sent.

So, out of earshot of the turning tides, beneath
the vast surface of the deep, a sea change hides.
With over-reaching mastery, dredging and netting,
we have laid waste the seas. With devilment

and microplastics (the word itself profanes
the world you worded) we are poisoning
each sea-spawned kind. We know this now, God help us.
Is nature's spirit, choked with plastic, spent?

*This poem responds to Gerard Manley Hopkins's poems 'The Sea and
the Skylark' and 'God's Grandeur'.*

The Sounds of Seagulls

On wings and chimney pots, all day
the urban seagulls squawk and squall.
With jagged shrieks and jaunty squeaks –
a dozen different kinds of call,
all meaningless to me – they keep
a lively conversation up,
while urban humans curse their greedy beaks.

Yet in my pensive quiet
they conjure
a seascape of the soul,
where aspirations soar and swoop,
cries from a troubled heart
converse with waves,
and rasping notes attain
a harmony with spume and spray.

Seagulls of the city,
set my heart at sea!
Tides are still your rhythms,
streetwise though you be.
Sing to me your shanties,
blustery and free!
Rough and raucous angels,
raise a prayer for me!

GOD

Seven Haiku

Truly to face God
without looking at oneself
facing God -- Jesus!

God is the tower
from which we see the land stretch
to infinity.

The circumference
and the centre are in God.
God circles the square.

Posing as righteous
even to myself I lie.
You are Otherwise.

God is the endlessly unexplored
garden
of the house where I belong.

Nothing is too hard
but there are ways that are too easy
even for God.

Sometimes all we want is
presence
and to no purpose.

God!

God is the word that in his absence
we have borrowed for our own purposes
not expecting him to need it again.
It has become one of our words
like love, power, security and hell.

God is not meant to signal his absence
but to remind ourselves
that we, having the use of it,
are still here so far.

Had we to halt silent at G-d
on the precipice of our words
we should abut
vertiginous space.

Hide and Seek

You are the hidden soul
of all that matters.
How could we miss you?

The secret saints,
the soulful ones –
they missed you
like a lost love,
inconsolable.
Wandering the world
they lost themselves
and hid
where you also hide.

To find you
they had only to whisper your name.
For you are always hidden,
always to be found
in agony among the olive trees
or where the agapanthus
sings your song.

Reconfiguring

Gather me, Shepherd, into one.
All truant thoughts that trail and stray,
all loves that linger –
call them home.
From cliffs and crannies of the mind
recover me.

Divine Optometrist, I look to you
to fix my wandering eyes
and focus me.
Clear me of cloud and cataract.
Revision me.

Search for me, Friend, in city streets
where I am aimless as a crowd
who cross and re-cross paths
till there is nowhere.
Here in the urban wilderness
find and re-friend me.

At the End of the Day

At the end of the long avenue of poplars –
a distant blur
I know to be a cottage.
There will be one lighted window,
sunflowers in a vase,
white wisteria around the porch.
I have only to touch the bell-pull.
You will be waiting.
I shall be home.